Let's Combat Micrographia®
Second Edition

Saba M. Shahid, M.S.

The Art Cart
www.smilethroughart.com
www.letscombatmicrographia.com

ISBN: 978-0-578-47881-4
ISBN-13: 978-0-578-47881-4

ISBN: 978-0-578-47881-4

Disclaimer:

This book is not intended as a substitute for the medical advice of physicians. The reader should regularly consult a physician in matters relating to his/her health and particularly with respect to any symptoms that may require diagnosis or medical attention.

Use of this book implies your acceptance of this disclaimer.

DEDICATION

To my amazing son, Aayan Ali, you are Mama's inspiration.

To my wonderful husband, Chad, thank you for making everything possible. Your drive and ambition motivate me and I am forever grateful for our journey together.

To my lovely parents, Ammie and Daddy, thank you for always supporting all of our endeavors.

To all the Parkinson's disease graduates of the Let's Combat Micrographia® Workshops, all the Smile Through Art® Workshop artists we have the privilege of working with, and to all those living with Parkinson's disease—here's to the start of living better with Parkinson's disease.

Always, in memory of Cindy Lynn Moir; you are our inspiration!

SMILE

CONTENTS

ACKNOWLEDGMENTS

The Art Cart would like to acknowledge the National Network of Libraries of Medicine, a branch of the U.S. National Institute of Health (NIH), that has supported the update to our book and the development of our Let's Combat Micrographia® Virtual Workshop and Training Program. The National Library of Medicine is the world's largest library and they have produced a nationally recognized medical database called MedlinePlus. MedlinePlus enables the general public to obtain credible and peer-reviewed information on diseases, conditions, and overall wellness. The website features directories, a medical encyclopedia, health information in different languages, extensive information on prescription and nonprescription drugs, and links to thousands of clinical trials. MedlinePlus is updated daily and can be accessed through www.medlineplus.gov.

Collaboration with the National Network of Libraries of Medicine has provided validation for our curriculum and training program, enabling us to make this resource available for people with Parkinson's disease and professionals who work with people living with Parkinson's disease.

We would like to acknowledge the support of and continued partnership with our fitness partner DopaFit® Parkinson's Movement Center. More information on DopaFit® can be found at www.DopaFit.com.

I

We would also like to acknowledge our Medical Advisory Board members who peer reviewed our book. The Medical Advisory Board consists of movement disorder specialists, occupational therapists, neurologists, and other professionals who have extensive years of experience working with the Parkinson's disease population.

The Let's Combat Micrographia® Medical Advisory Board includes the following individuals:

- Chad Moir, President of DopaFit®
- Dr. Marie-Helene Saint-Hilaire, Movement Disorder Specialist
- Dr. Kara Smith, Movement Disorder Specialist
- Dr. Anindita Deb, Movement Disorder Specialist
- Dr. Umer Akbar, Movement Disorder Specialist
- Dr. Elizabeth Budman, Movement Disorder Specialist
- Cathi Thomas, RN, MS, CNRN
- Cally Donahue, OTD, MS, OTR/L
- Amanda Landsbaum, MS, OTR/L

About Let's Combat Micrographia®

Very limited information on micrographia is readily available to the public. Since 2014, we have worked closely with people living with PD to understand micrographia and have developed techniques that work to improve this symptom. Our **Let's Combat Micrographia® Workshops** is the only research based program in the world that focuses specifically on how to improve small handwriting while increasing confidence in the process of writing.

⌨ **Web Extra:** Find out more about our training program and how you can sign up by watching our online YouTube video, https://www.youtube.com/watch?v=lXWmnH5TlyE or visit www.letscombatmicrographia.com.

This edition of the interactive workbook is an update to the previously published 2016 edition and is based on our past three years of work assessing micrographia with the PD population. This edition has three times more content including how writing and exercise techniques can improve handwriting. With this book, our goal is to help improve your handwriting and take control of the micrographia symptom. This is an **interactive** book that will require you to write, do exercises, be patient, and do lots of practice exercises. You will soon see that with dedication many improvements can be made to your micrographia.

If you would like to go one step further in your journey of improving micrographia, attend our **Let's Combat**

Micrographia® Virtual Workshop from the comfort of your home. You will go through an instructor-led, six-week course that will teach you how to improve your handwriting using many of the techniques discussed in this book. Below are two images of a participant that completed the Virtual Workshop series. Here is a change in their handwriting in just three days!

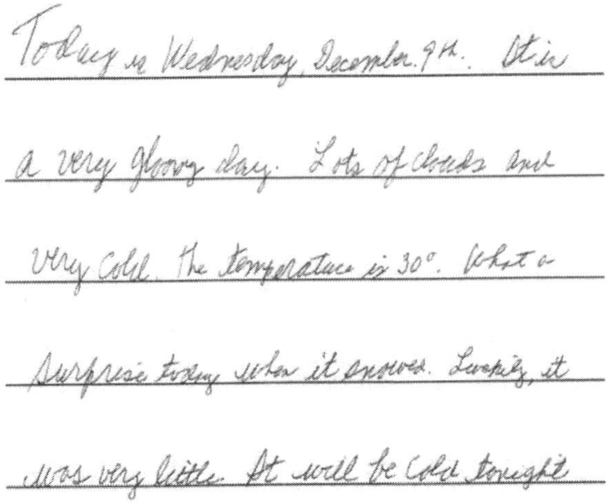
Today is Wednesday, December 9th. It is
a very gloomy day. Lots of clouds and
very cold. The temperature is 30°. What a
surprise today when it snows. Luckily, it
was very little. It will be cold tonight

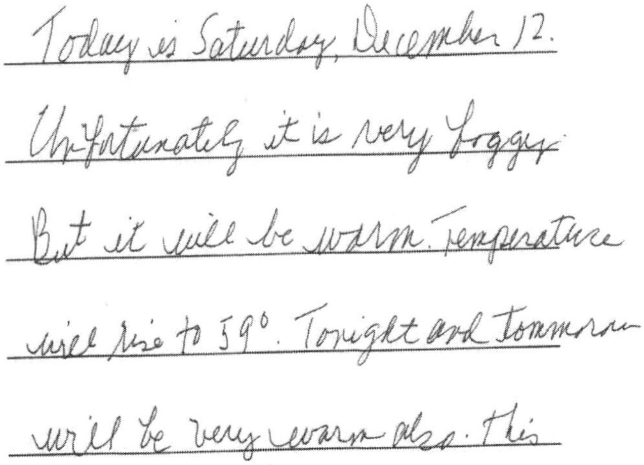
Today is Saturday, December 12.
Unfortunately it is very foggy.
But it will be warm. Temperature
will rise to 59°. Tonight and Tommorow
will be very warm also. This

A separate training program is also available for professionals working with people living with PD who would like to teach our copyrighted material to their community of people living with Parkinson's disease.

For more information on our programming, to learn how to host a Let's Combat Micrographia® Workshop or to sign up for our Let's Combat Micrographia® Virtual Workshop, please visit our website www.letscombatmicrographia.com

LETS COMBAT MICROGRAPHIA: SECOND EDITION

[illegible]

My n am is Ange Palm[illegible] [illegible]

[illegible] ?

About The Art Cart

The Let's Combat Micrographia® program was developed by The Art Cart. The Art Cart is an internationally recognized creativity and movement program that focuses on **spreading SMILEs and healing through art and movement** to populations that list the **"inability to smile"** as a symptom of their disease. Facial masking, or the inability to smile, is a common symptom that goes unnoticed and is misinterpreted in those living with Parkinson's disease (PD). Therefore, we have made it our mission to travel to various PD communities to educate and teach the benefits of creativity, movement, and smiling for people living with PD. Through our specially designed Smile Through Art® Workshop curriculum, we enhance mood and creativity while combating micrographia and strengthening fine and gross motor movements to teach our participants how to **live better with Parkinson's**. Our research proves that **96%** of the time, participants with PD have a positive change in mood after participating in a Smile Through Art® Workshop. This research has been published in the *Journal of Alzheimer's Disease and Parkinsonism*.

We call ourselves "The Art Cart" to be accessible to the greater PD population. To achieve this goal, we travel to cities internationally to bring our workshops to various PD communities. Since 2014, we have traveled to more than 30 states and internationally.

Achievements

The Art Cart was featured in the October 2018 issue of *Brain & Life* magazine. The Art Cart was featured at the 2016 Global Education Summit on Neurology and Psychiatry and was selected to present at a Renewal Room at the 2016 World Parkinson's Congress. Over the years, The Art Cart has participated in numerous conferences, organizational walks, and events for PD, including rallying at Capitol Hill to raise awareness about the disease.

Let's Combat Micrographia® Edition 1 and Edition 2 books were also be featured at the 2019 World Parkinson's Congress in Kyoto, Japan.

We work internationally with different Parkinson's organizations, hospitals, clinics, Parkinson's Disease Centers, nursing homes, and assisted living centers. Please contact us to learn more about how you can bring our programming to your PD community.

You can also find us on Facebook at www.facebook.com/smilethroughart and Instagram, @smilethroughart

1
What Is Micrographia?

The prefix, "micro" means small, and the suffix "graphia" refers to writing; when you put the two words together, you get "micrographia" or small handwriting. Did you know about micrographia prior to getting this book? If not, have no fear; we will teach you all you need to know about this symptom and how to improve it!

Micrographia is a common symptom of Parkinson's disease and is referred to as a *prodromal symptom* because it is a symptom that indicates the start of a disease. Although micrographia often appears before any other symptoms are noticed, it is one of the last symptoms many living with Parkinson's disease learn of.

Micrographia causes many to stop writing and instead depend on their spouse or care partner to write for them. Simple things like writing a check become more difficult due to the decline of dopamine, a neurotransmitter found to be deficient in those with Parkinson's disease. Fine muscle control is impacted, and rigidity is increased, making a task such as writing seem impossible to accomplish.

People living with Parkinson's disease that are impacted by micrographia have handwriting that looks cramped, slanted, or tilted, and individual letters tend to be smaller than normal.

Words are typically spaced closer together making it harder to read. Below is a writing example from a person who has Parkinson's with micrographia:

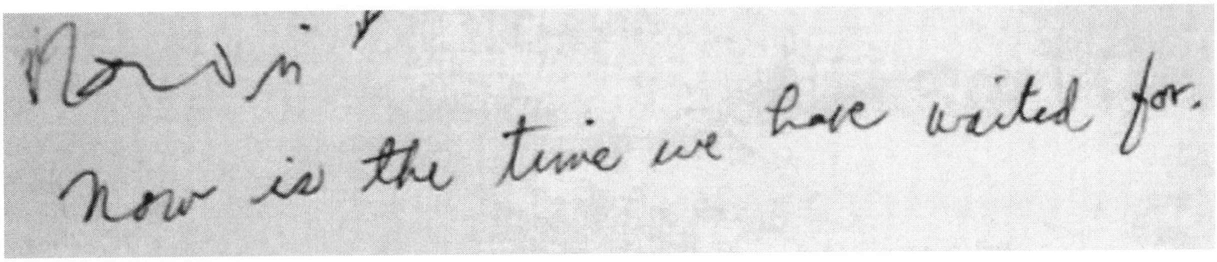
Now is the time we have waited for.

The good news is, with some practice, symptoms of micrographia can be controlled and improved. If you are living with micrographia, with the help of this book, you will soon be able to start depending on yourself again to write those checks or sign an important document.

This workbook will introduce you to a series of writing exercises and hand exercises, as well as tools you can use to assist in your handwriting. Moreover, it will teach you how to work with your micrographia symptom instead of working against it. **Let's learn how to do this and how to combat micrographia!**

If you choose to participate in our online Let's Combat Micrographia® course, you can improve your writing in as little as six weeks as shown in the picture on the next page. Be inspired by this picture, and know that with this workbook and some help from us, your handwriting will improve!

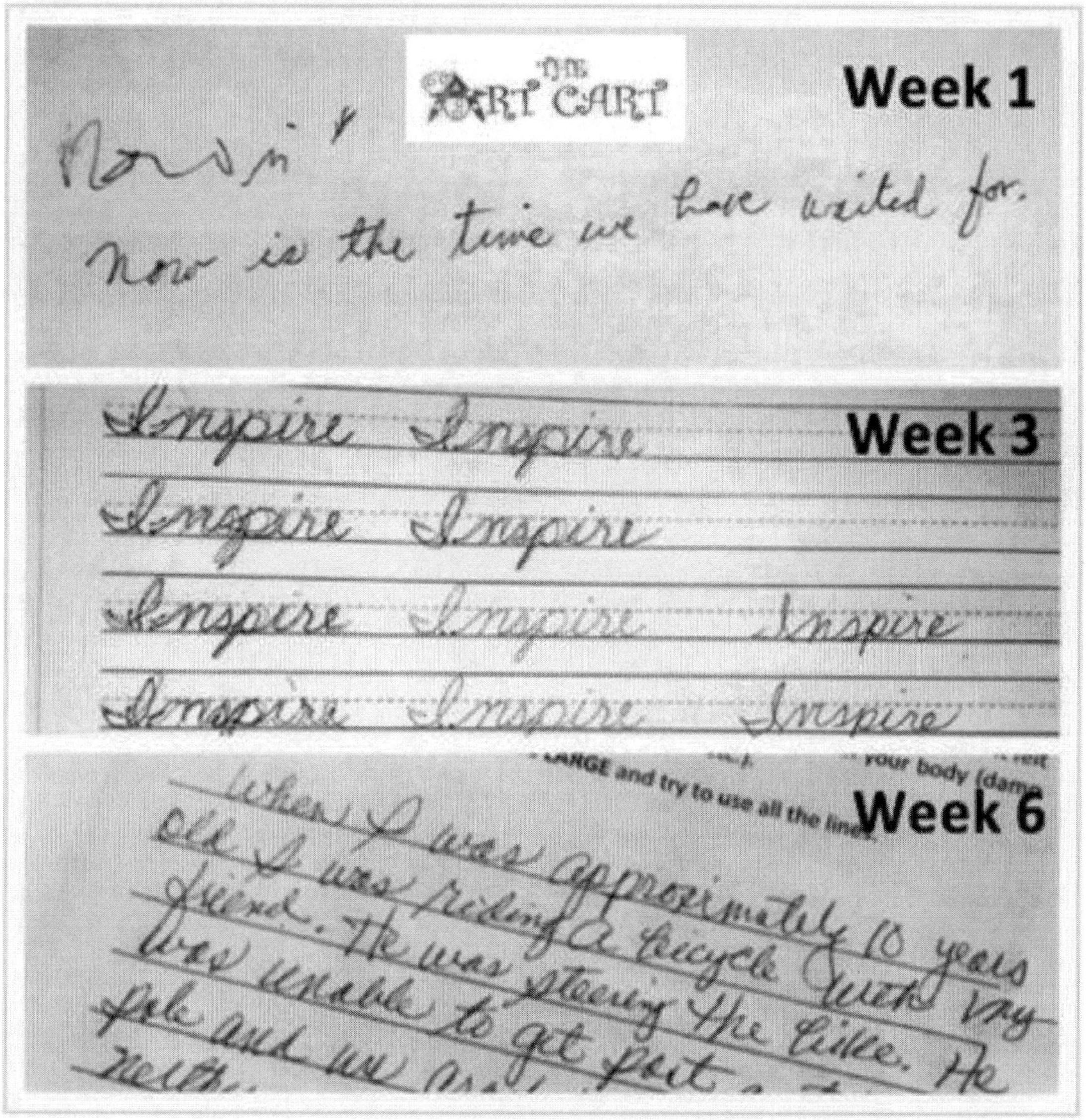
THE ART CART
Week 1
now is the time we have waited for.
Week 3
Inspire Inspire
Inspire Inspire
Inspire Inspire Inspire
Inspire Inspire Inspire
Week 6

2
Mind-Body Reeducation

Remember, improving anything and becoming better requires practice, a positive mind-set, and perseverance. Using the tools in this interactive workbook, you will need to practice *deliberately,* meaning with the intention and purpose to make your handwriting better. Deliberate practice is a special type of practice that requires focused attention to improve overall writing. It requires your mind and body to be in sync and fully dedicated to the task at hand.

How can you achieve this? What is the best way to practice deliberately and reeducate yourself? Create a goal, and set aside a specific time and place to work on this workbook every day. Create a **routine** and avoid all disruptions. An example routine plan is provided below:

- **Goal**: Improve my handwriting
- **Frequency**: Every day
- **Time**: from 10am to 11am, after taking my morning medication
- **Place**: Kitchen island

Now write down what *your* routine will be:

- Goal: _____ Improve my handwriting _____
- Frequency: _____ Everyday _____
- Time: _____ 10am-11am _____
- Place: _____ Desk _____

From extensive experience working with people living with Parkinson's disease, we noticed the best writing performance occurs in an "on" period. During an "on" period, a person with Parkinson's disease can move with ease and often with a decreased presence of tremors and stiffness. "Off" periods, on the other hand, describe those times when a person with Parkinson's has greater difficulty with movement. Therefore, for optimal performance, we recommend practicing your writing while in your "on" periods, which for many is thirty minutes to an hour after taking medication.

Moreover, while you are practicing deliberately, we'll also be retraining your mind and body. While you are working on improving your handwriting, we will be focused on improving your movement and overall posture (fingers, wrist, hand, arm, shoulder). These elements combined together assist in improving your overall micrographia.

3
Starting from the Basics

Before we get into the details of combating micrographia, it's important that you **seize** this opportunity in front of you now. Like any new task, you will have to start from the basics, be **patient** with yourself, and work toward mastering the art of handwriting again. So, keep an open mind, and do your best to repeat as many of the techniques discussed in the chapters to come.

As children, we were taught how to write early on in classrooms. As grade levels progressed, so did our handwriting. This positive correlation developed neat, parallel, readable, and almost perfect writing. Some methods of teaching that were most likely used were free writing, tracing, dot-to-dot writing, and exploring different types of writing, such as cursive and printing.

Those living with Parkinson's disease are put at square one again, so we have to **start with the basics**. We will explore some of the techniques mentioned above and many others in the chapters that follow. Consider this workbook practice as part of reeducating yourself on the art of handwriting!

4
Warm Up to Work Out

Before doing any type of exercise, you need to warm up your muscles to prepare your body for what is to come. Imagine you are watching a football game, and your favorite team is about to go on the field. Chances are that before the game starts, they are warming up on the sidelines using techniques that will get them ready to play. We will be doing the same before every writing session. Get your favorite writing instrument ready because we are going onto the writing field and giving it our best shot!

We will be teaching you various exercises throughout this workbook. When you see the words, *Exercise Break*, you will complete the exercise that is explained. Always make sure to consult with your physician before trying any of the exercises we mention.

Let's start with a simple warm-up:

Exercise Break 1: Before we can get into the beginning exercises, make sure you are seated in a comfortable seat, with your back against the chair, being mindful of your posture. Place your feet flat on the floor. Practice rolling your shoulders. Roll both shoulders forward 10 times and then backward 10 times. Count out loud while rolling your shoulders. Now, roll the shoulder of the hand you write with forward and backward 10 times. This is warming up your shoulder and arm while getting you prepared to write.

Another very important thing to be mindful of is where your writing arm, wrist, and hand are placed in relation to the table you are working on. The ideal table will be at elbow height. You want to make sure your hand, wrist, and arm are all supported by the table. As you can see in the image below, the hand, wrist, and arm are all supported and resting on the table. Proper placement of your arm will allow you to feel more comfortable when writing. For left-handed writers, it may be easiest to slightly slant the paper as shown in the image below.

5
The Right Fit

After posture, the next step is to select a writing instrument that feels comfortable to you, such as a pen, pencil, felt pen, marker, and so on. Many ergonomic writing aids are available, such as pen and pencil grips, that will allow for an easier hold. Ring pens are another aid that provides more stability and control by allowing you to place your index finger into a ring that is a part of the pen. Below are images of three writing aids that we use in our workshops. These are highly rated by our previous Let's Combat Micrographia® Parkinson's participants. These aids can be used on pens or pencils and provide additional surface area for you to rest your fingers on, making the act of holding a writing instrument less burdensome.

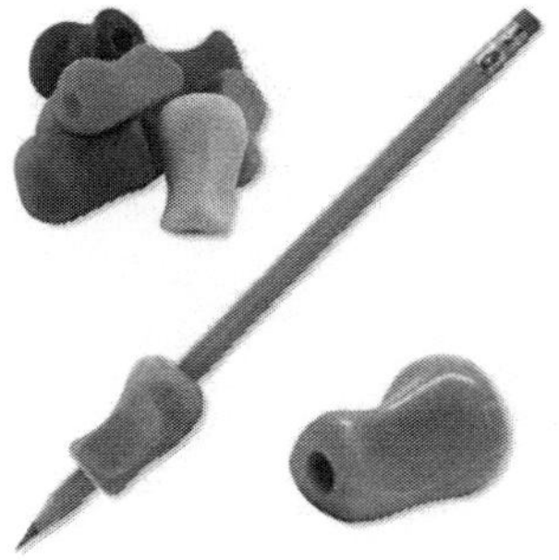

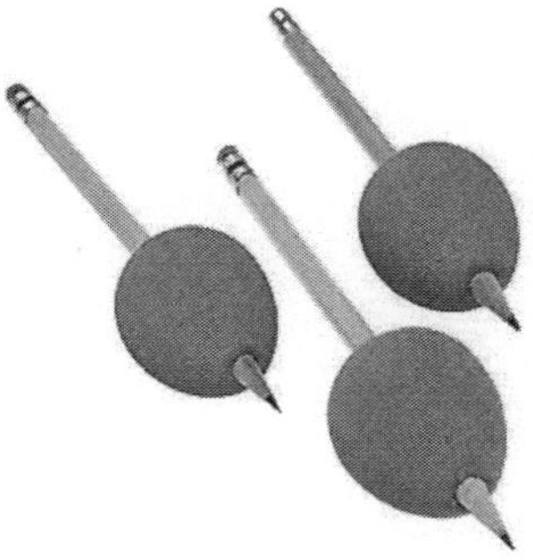

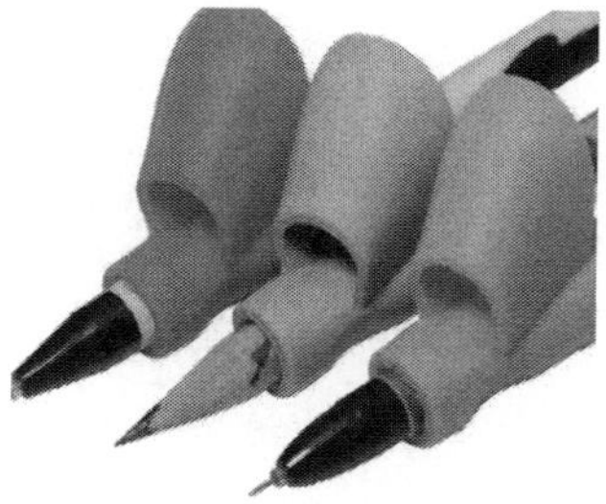

Another great option is using a weighted hand glove. If your hand tremors, this will help decrease the tremor to some extent because weight is being placed on your hand. Before purchasing a weighted hand glove, however, make sure there is an adequate amount of weight in the glove (at least one to two pounds).

Finally, the last option that has been rated highly by our past Let's Combat Micrographia® graduates is a weighted pen. This option is more expensive but does work very well and can be used both on pens and pencils.

As you can see, many options are available, but it is all about finding the right fit for yourself! What may feel comfortable to one person may not feel comfortable for another. Try as many options as possible because the more confident you feel with your writing instrument, the better you will do. To make it easier for you, the ergonomic aids listed above are available for purchase on our website, www.letscombatmicrographia.com. You can try just one or purchase all through our combo pack option.

Do your best to try as many as you can in order to find **the right fit**! After you find the one for you, try to stick with this writing instrument for the duration of this workbook and writing course. You will find that the more you use it, the more comfortable and confident you will feel.

6
Think BIG!

Hopefully, by now, you have selected your primary writing instrument.

Let's try something!

Exercise Break 2: Hold your writing instrument in the hand that you write with. Imagine your paper is in front of you in the air instead of on the table. Your paper is the size of a large poster board, and your job is to exaggerate your letters so that each letter touches both the top and bottom of the poster board. As an example (if you are right-handed), when making the letter A, start at your left elbow (bottom of the poster board), go past your head (top of the poster board), and back down to the height of your right elbow (bottom of the poster board). Now that was a BIG A! If you are left-handed, you will start the A at your right elbow. Go through the entire alphabet in the same manner.

💻 **Web Extra:** Our Let's Combat Micrographia® Virtual Workshop includes a video on this exercise.

How did that feel? Did you move your entire arm, or were you simply moving your wrist in the air?

Please explain:

_____

_____

_____

Do you think you can do that better? Let's try it again! Remember use BIG letters, practice good posture, and move your entire arm.

Repeat *Exercise Break 2*.

After repeating *Exercise Break 2*, how did you feel? How did the motion of *Exercise Break 2* feel? Did you move your entire arm, or were you simply moving your wrist in the air?

Please explain:

_____

_____

_____

Not only was that an exercise for you to write your alphabet large and BIG, but it was also an exercise for your arm. Chances are your writing arm is feeling a bit fatigued right now. This may seem like a simple exercise, but it requires thought, concentration (Thinking BIG), and large movements (Writing BIG).

Writing in the air most likely felt odd simply because this is not something you are used to doing. It put you in an uncomfortable position, which is completely okay. You have to get used to feeling uncomfortable because relearning the art of writing is going to feel uncomfortable at the beginning. With practice and patience, it will start feeling more comfortable.

Why is it important to Think BIG? This exercise is important because it will start training your mind to deliberately write larger while breaking through the limitations of micrographia. We are going to continue working toward Thinking BIG and Writing BIG. **Remember, large (BIG) thoughts bring BIG action!**

⌨ **Web Extra:** Our Let's Combat Micrographia® Virtual Workshop includes a video on the additional benefits of Thinking BIG and Writing BIG.

7
Linear

Now that you have practiced in the air, let's put those motions you were making to the test! How straight can you get? Writing in a straight line while holding a writing instrument can be a very difficult task for those living with Parkinson's disease. One thing that can help prepare your hands and fingers for grasping a writing instrument is to perform hand stretches prior to starting your writing. Just like any other muscle in the body, the muscles in your forearm and palm require a warm-up to effectively move your fingers. For many of the people with Parkinson's we have had the privilege of working with, writing is an activity that has not been done in a while. Therefore, let's prepare our hands and fingers by performing a quick stretch we call the **PD Finger Extension**.

Exercise Break 3: Sitting with good posture, place your hands flat on a table and keep your fingers next to each other so they are touching. Now, separate your fingers and open them as wide as you can, allowing each finger to be far from the finger next to it. Leave your fingers open for 10 seconds, and then bring your fingers back into the touching position. Do this exercise ten times on each hand, stretching your hands as far as they can go.

The image on the next page will help you visualize this exercise.

⌨ **Web Extra:** Our Let's Combat Micrographia® Virtual Workshop includes a video on this exercise.

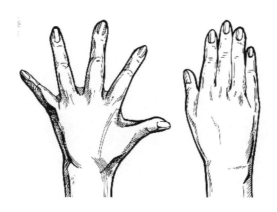

Open (Separated)   Closed (Touching)

This writing exercise also helps you with controlling your writing instrument and relearning ways to maneuver it around to make letters. Other benefits include the development of prewriting skills, such as practicing holding and using your writing instrument.

As we mentioned earlier in this chapter, writing in a straight line while holding a writing instrument can be a very difficult task. Letters are all different shapes and sizes. Some are curved, while others are jagged and straight. For this reason, before starting to write letters on paper, let's work on retraining the mind on the different shapes and sizes of letters by tracing over various lines.

To begin, use the lines below and trace over them using your writing hand.

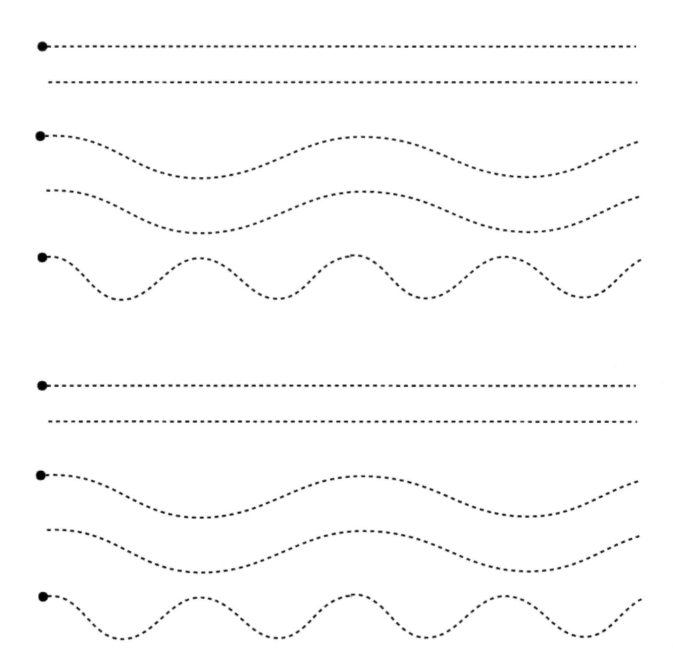

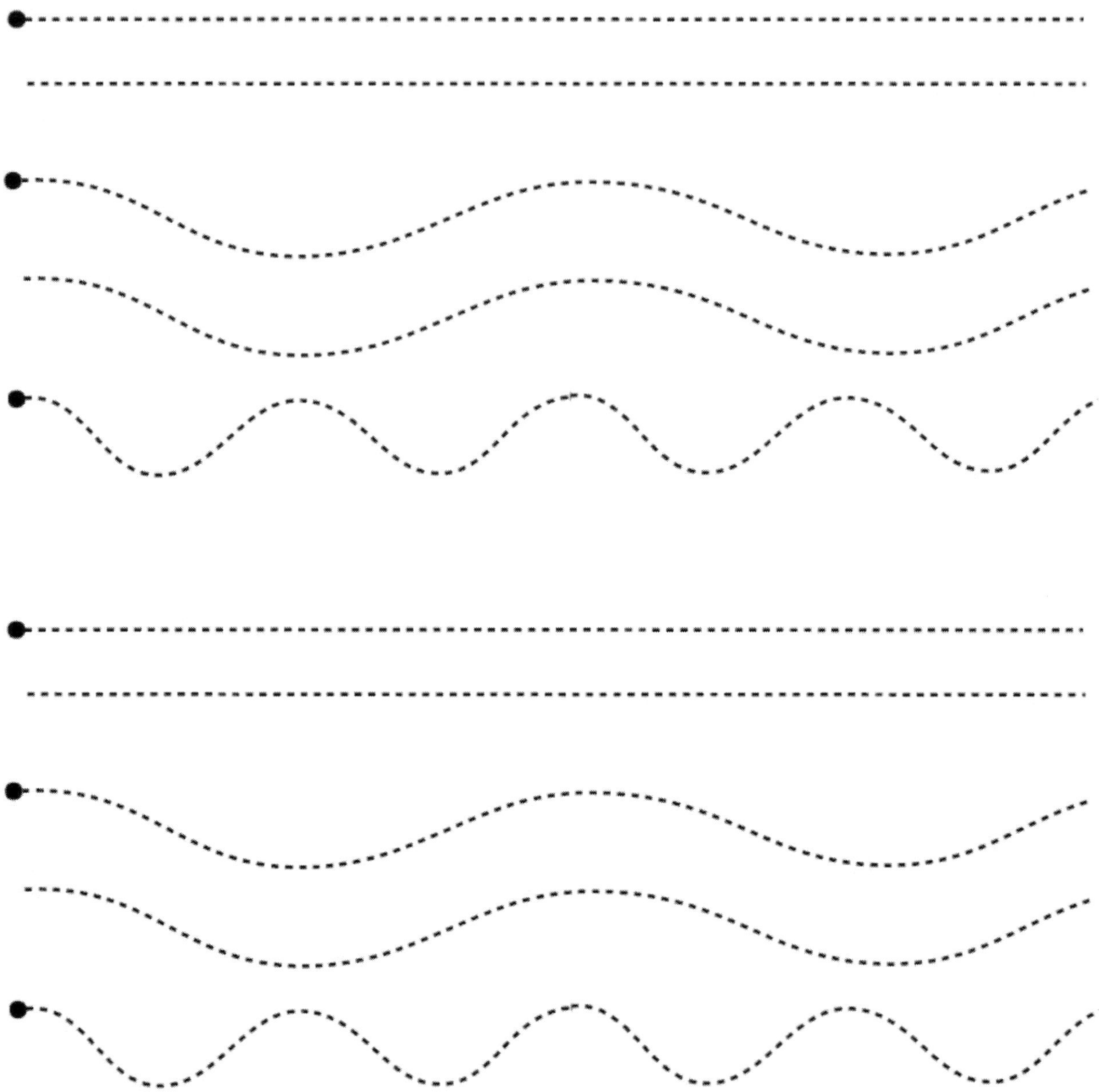

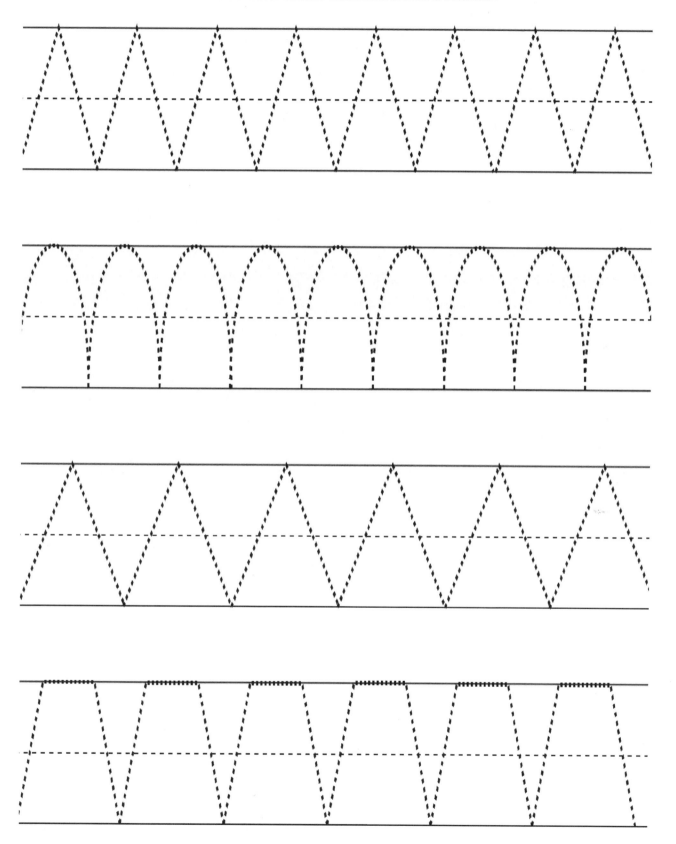

Well done! You just went through several different patterns of lines. Horizontal and vertical lines help make the letters E, F, H, and I, whereas slanted lines help make the letters A, V, M, and W. Curved lines help write the letters C, O, and U.

While you were tracing, if you noticed your hands shuffling instead of tracing the line in a constant movement, you are relying on your wrist too much. Instead, try engaging your shoulder, arm, forearm, **and** wrist as we discussed in Chapter 4. Rolling your shoulder back and sitting with proper posture will help facilitate engaging your entire arm. Be sure to focus on engaging your entire arm, and combat these lines as one continuous movement.

Now repeat the exercise you just completed above by tracing the same lines provided below. Remember use good posture, and support that writing hand!

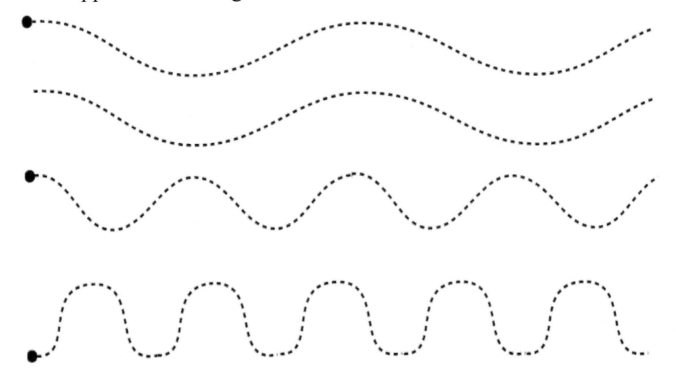

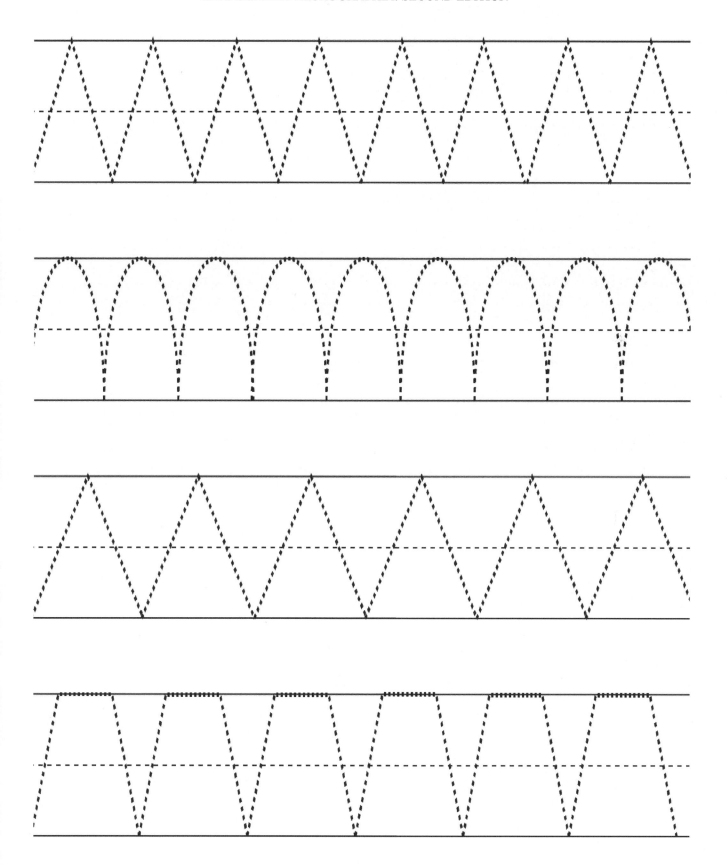

How did you do? Did you feel more confident in tracing the lines as you progressed from page to page?

Please explain:

_____

_____

_____

8
Paper

The average size of the space in each line of lined paper is 8.7mm—just .034th of an inch! In other words, this space is very, very, very small. If you ask a person with Parkinson's disease to combat their already small handwriting using this type of paper, it will be nearly impossible to see any improvement! For this reason, we encourage using wider lined paper as you see below:

Our Let's Combat Micrographia® Journal contains an entire section with wide lined paper. We also have several lined paper templates available for download via our Virtual Workshop series that have proven to be beneficial in combating micrographia.

9
Macro-graphia

We have talked about Thinking BIG, and now you have to actually put that thought into action. When combating micrographia, you want to do the opposite of "micro"-graphia. The key is to exaggerate your writing. Make it BIG, large, or "**macro**." From here on out, we want you to retrain your mind to think that you have **macro**-graphia not micrographia.

As mentioned in the previous chapter, using a paper with larger spaced lines is beneficial. Therefore, the best way to put the Think BIG mantra into action is to start writing on paper that has larger spaced lines. Lines are your friends! You will see that writing tends to be easier when lines are provided. The lines will help keep you from steering off the page. In a perfect world, we would have lines all the time. However, this is not always the case, so practicing with lines now will help you when you have no lines to work with.

Encourage yourself. Allow your letters to touch from the bottom to the top of the line. A helpful tip is to verbally tell yourself, **"Think BIG, write MACRO."** If you remind yourself and believe you can, you will! Verbal cues will remind you to write larger and will help you be more alert and conscious. In our Virtual Workshop series, our instructors provide verbal cues.

This is one of the reasons why using our Virtual Workshop will help you learn more quickly and see faster improvement.

To begin, practice writing the letters A through Z using the lines provided below. The first letter has been done for you to show that you have to go from the bottom of the line to the top of the line. As you write each letter, say it **aloud**. Saying your letters out loud exercises your vocal cords. You may or may not know that softened speech is another symptom of Parkinson's disease. Therefore, take advantage of this task and say these letters **loud and proud**.

We always encourage our participants to be as loud as they can when given the opportunity. Whether at an exercise class or while completing this book, when you have the chance to exercise your vocal cords, take advantage of it and push yourself to be loud.

As you begin writing the alphabet, remember to say the letter and **then** write the letter, repeating this until you get to Z. For this writing exercise, write in all capital letters.

_____

_____

How did you do? If all of your letters are not touching both the top line and the bottom line, you did not challenge yourself enough!

Please explain:

_____

_____

_____

Let's repeat this again, and this time, **Think BIG, Write MACRO**, and speak louder than you did! Continue this writing exercise by writing capital letters.

Let's put those pens or pencils down and take a quick finger exercise break. In earlier chapters, we stretched our shoulders, forearms, hands, and palm muscles. Now it's time to put our fingers to the test! From the results of our Let's Combat Micrographia® Workshops, the exercise below is shown to improve fine motor control.

Exercise Break 4: We like to call this next exercise the **PD Finger Tapping exercise**. Imagine that the two circles on the next page are two paint dots: one gray and the other black. Your goal here is to exercise your fingers by simultaneously tapping a different finger on each dot.

- To begin, start with your right hand. Place your index finger on the gray dot, and place your middle finger on the black dot. Now, lift your index finger off the gray dot while placing your middle finger on the black dot. Bring your index finger back onto the gray dot while lifting your middle finger off the black dot. Repeat this tapping motion ten times, counting to ten out loud.
- Next, perform the same exercise, but this time, place your index finger on the gray dot and your ring finger on the black dot. Count to 10 out loud.
- Repeat again by placing your index finger on the gray dot and pinky on the black dot. Count to 10 out loud.
- Lastly, place your thumb on the gray dot and your pinky on the black dot. Count to 10 out loud.

Now repeat again using your left hand. Start with your index finger on the black dot and your middle finger on the gray dot. Then, repeat with your index finger on the black dot and ring finger on the gray dot. Continue until you finish with your pinky and thumb.

You will complete 40 taps per hand in this one exercise. That is a total of 80 taps and a great way to get each individual finger warmed up and ready for not only holding the writing instrument but also for the act of writing itself.

PD Finger Tapping brought to you by The Art Cart

🖥 **Web Extra:** Our Let's Combat Micrographia® Virtual Workshop includes a video on this PD Finger Tapping exercise.

Now that your fingers are stretched, let's repeat this writing exercise a few more times:

A

10
From Letters To Words

Another tip on exaggerating your writing is to write on a whiteboard or chalkboard, which is beneficial because it encourages gross motor movement. If you exaggerate your writing on a blackboard, you are forced to move not only your hand but your entire arm!

Now let's put letters together to form words! The Art Cart's SMILE acronym stands for **Seize your day, Make positive memories, Inspire yourself and others, Love, and Promote a healthy environment.** You will practice writing these words in both print form and cursive form.

Here is an extra challenge: while you are writing these words, think of things that you have done to fulfill the **SMILE** acronym. As an example, you seized your day by reading through this book and taking an interactive approach!

Use the arrows provided in each word to coordinate the movement of your writing instrument. Use the blank spaces provided to write the word after you finish tracing it.

Smile Smile
Smile Smile
Smile Smile
Smile Smile
Smile Smile
Smile Smile
Smile Smile
Smile Smile

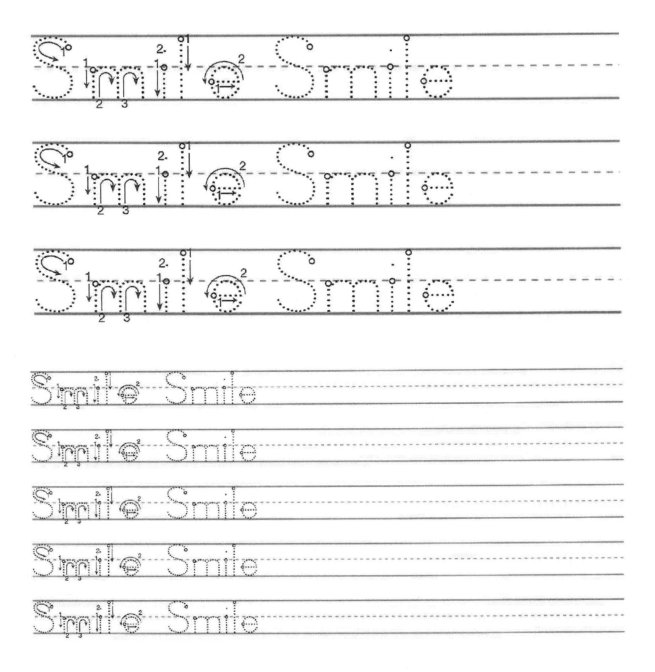

Did you notice how we went from a larger font to a smaller font and a larger space to a smaller space? This trains your mind to naturally write larger but also to be confident in the writing process if a smaller space is provided.

Before you try another word, let's repeat ***Exercise Break 2*** found in Chapter 5. Write the word *Positive* in the air before writing it on each line below. You will **repeat** writing in the air each time before tracing the letters below.

Let's begin:

Positive Positive
Positive Positive
Positive Positive

Positive Memories Positive Memories
Positive Memories Positive Memories
Positive Memories Positive Memories
Positive Memories Positive Memories

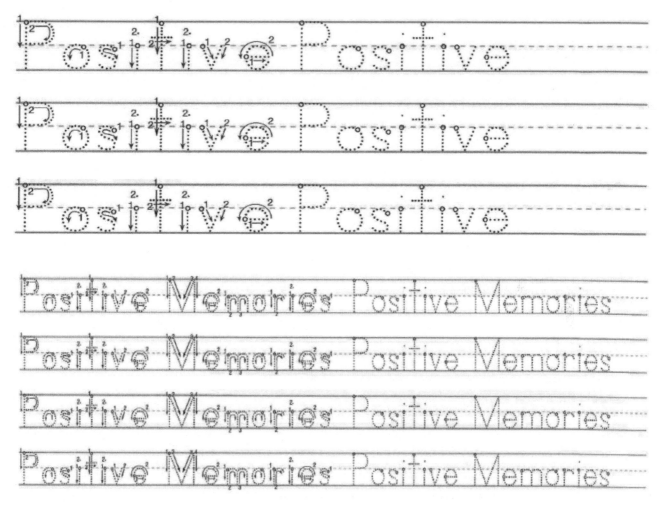

After repeating ***Exercise Break 2*** and completing the tracing above, how did it feel to write in the air and then write the word? Did you feel that you wrote MACRO because you exaggerated the word in the air before writing it on the paper?

Please explain:

_____

_____

_____

To review, in this chapter, we are employing the same methodology you learned about in Chapter 6 and Chapter 9. Writing MACRO or larger will help you see improvements in your micrographia. Let's work on writing MACRO with our alphabet again:

_____

A _____

_____

_____

11
Print versus Cursive

You may be asking yourself why we are working on both print and cursive. These two forms of writing are the most popular. While print is a bit easier to practice with, cursive offers other challenges. When writing in cursive, you have to be very mindful not to write too small as this style of writing naturally has the letters placed closer together, which may make your writing look narrow and slanted.

In the work that we have done with people living with Parkinson's disease, **improving handwriting is easiest using the print method because there is more room to write, and letters can be made larger in an easier fashion**. Additionally, when printing, you are focusing on each letter of the word individually; cursive, on the other hand, requires you to be mindful of connecting each of the letters.

Of course, you should practice whichever method comes most naturally to you. Let's work on practicing both to see which you prefer.

Start with print and then finish with cursive using the word on the next page:

Inspire Inspire

Inspire Inspire

Inspire Inspire

Inspire Inspire

Inspire Inspire

Inspire Inspire

Inspire Inspire

Inspire Inspire

Let’s try another word:

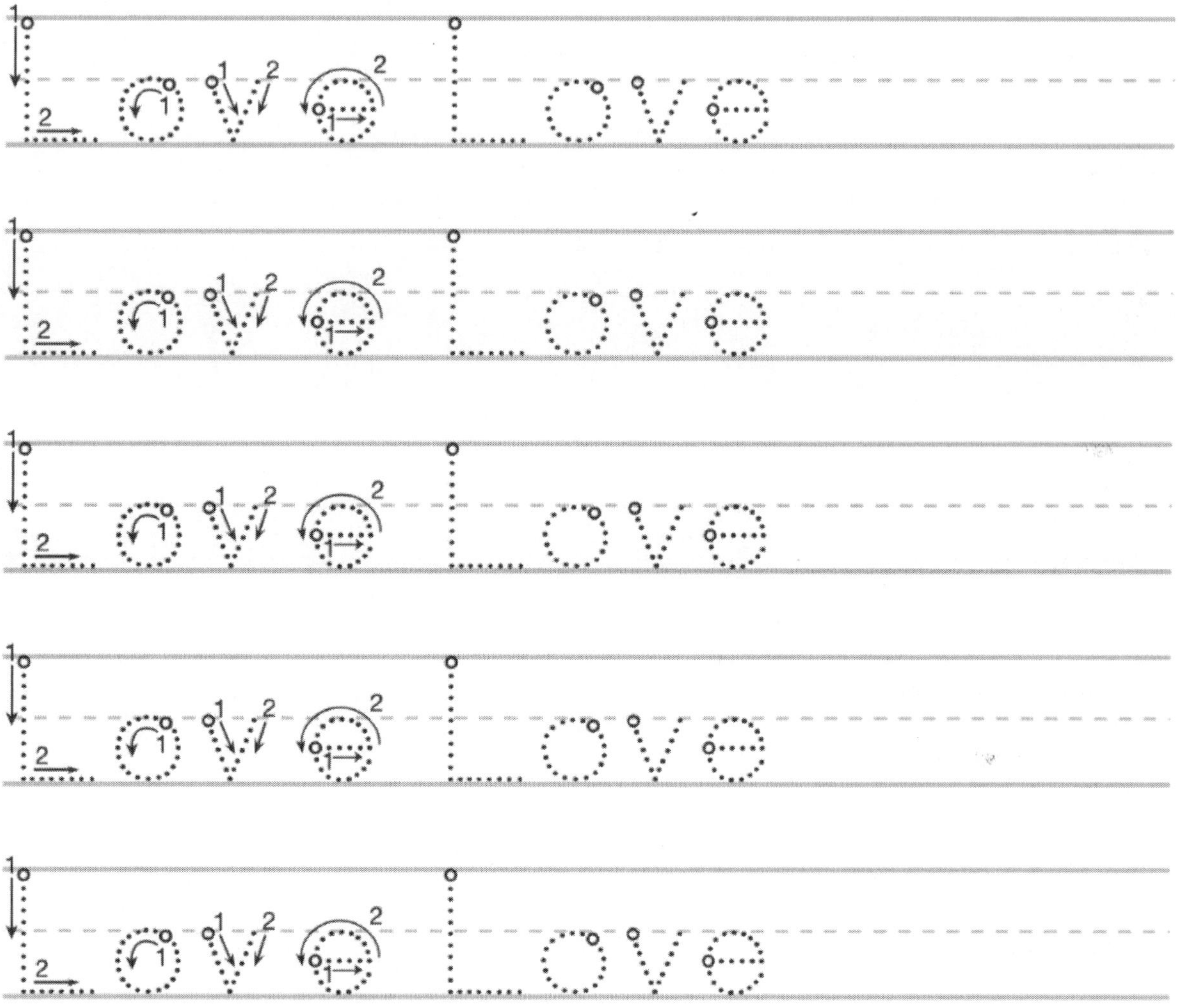
Love Love
Love Love
Love Love
Love Love
Love Love

Love Love

Love Love

Love Love

Love Love

Love Love

Which style of writing did you like better? Why? Please explain:

_____

_____

_____

_____

_____

12
Numbers

Practicing numbers is just as important as practicing letters and forming them into words. Numbers are used often, particularly with writing checks. Go through each of the lines containing numbers below, and then use the last line to practice writing the number without using the tracing method.

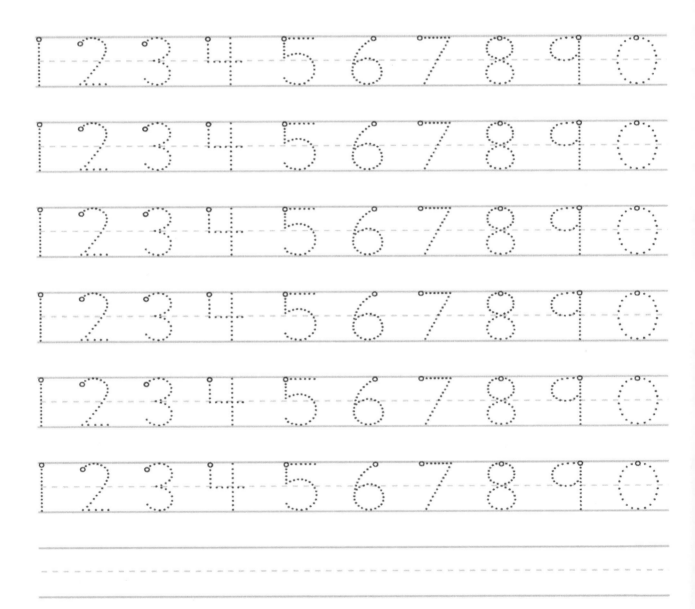

Similar to how we practice writing our letters MACRO, now let's practice our numbers. Write numbers 1 through 20 on the lines below:

_____

_____

_____

_____

Write out the following words into numbers:

1. Ten _____

2. Five Hundred _____

3. Twenty-Six _____

4. One Million _____

5. Nine Hundred and Seventy-Two _____

6. Forty-Three_____

7. Six Thousand Eight Hundred and Eleven_____

8. Zero_____

9. One Million Seven Hundred Thousand_____

10. Three Hundred and Fifteen_____

1 2 3 4 5 6 7 8 9 0

1 2 3 4 5 6 7 8 9 0

13
Focused Practice Makes Perfect

Now, imagine writing on a canvas with a paintbrush in your hand instead of a pen. Your goal is to paint the entire canvas with words. Don't have a paintbrush and canvas? Don't worry! The pages that follow are your canvas. They include various writing exercises and prompts for you to work on.

A few reminders before you tackle the pages that are to come:

- Remember to **stretch** your hands before starting any writing exercise. Repeat any and all of the hand exercises we mention in this book.
- Remember to create a **routine** by picking a specific place to work on your handwriting. Creating a routine by also picking a specific time of day when you take out this workbook to **focus** on improving your handwriting.
- Pick a writing instrument that you feel **comfortable** with.
- **Write as much as you can.** Push yourself to improve.
- **Think BIG, Write MACRO, and Speak LOUD.**

Writing Prompt 1: Describe a positive memorable event and how it felt to you, but do not name the feeling. Instead, tell how it felt in your body (damp hands, sweet taste, wobbly knees, etc.).

Do your best to make your letters **MACRO,** and try to use all the lines.

_____

_____

_____

_____

_____

_____

_____

Writing Prompt 2: Use the words listed below to create a story. Each word must be used at least once and in separate sentences.

Smile	Listen	House	Banana	Ice cream
Sparkle	Sunny	Wonderful	Crown	Giraffe

_____

_____

_____

_____

_____

_____

_____

Writing Prompt 3: Trace over the words below, and then complete the following thought by explaining how you promote a healthy environment (exercise, positive thinking, family time, YOU time, etc.). Do your best to write more than five sentences for this prompt!

I promote a

healthy

environment in my

life by doing the

following...

Writing Prompt 4: Practice your numbers and check writing by writing on the checks below.

_____

1280

Date _____

Pay to the
Order of _____ $ [ ]

_____ Dollars

For _____   _____

-:453337642-:5543765435212 1280

_____

1281

Date _____

Pay to the
Order of _____ $ [ ]

_____ Dollars

For _____   _____

-:453337642-:5543765435212 1281

14
Next Steps

Congratulations! You've made it to the end of this workbook! Now you have the knowledge, tools, as well as hand and writing exercises you need to improve your handwriting. Be sure to practice, practice, practice, and go through this workbook again. Remember, improving handwriting takes time and is an ongoing effort. We published an additional resource, the Let's Combat Micrographia® Journal, for you to continue practicing your handwriting. This can be purchased on our website, www.letscombatmicrographia.com

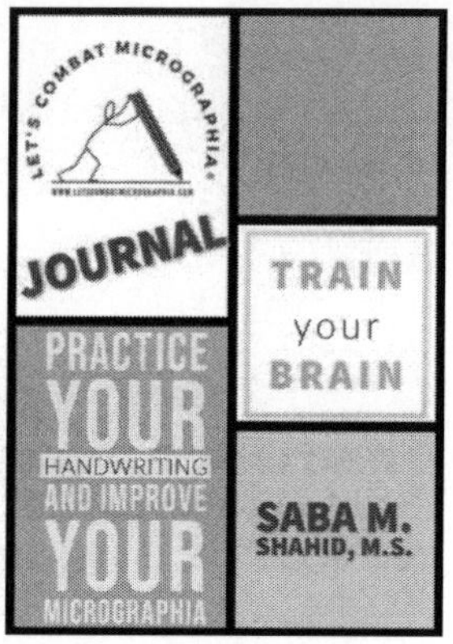
LET'S COMBAT MICROGRAPHIA
JOURNAL
TRAIN
your
BRAIN
PRACTICE
YOUR
HANDWRITING
AND IMPROVE
YOUR
MICROGRAPHIA
SABA M.
SHAHID, M.S.

If you want to take your practice one step further, we highly encourage you to enroll in our **Let's Combat Micrographia® Virtual Workshop series**. In this Virtual Workshop series, you will be challenged even further, learn additional writing and hand exercises for improvement, and get access to videos that demonstrate these and other writing and hand exercises. You will have homework to complete and upon successful completion you will also receive a certificate after successfully passing the course!

To sign up for the **Let's Combat Micrographia® Virtual Workshop series,** visit www.letscombatmicrographia.com.

15
Glossary of Terms and Other Resources

Dopamine: A brain chemical used by nerve cells to help control muscle movement. With Parkinson's disease, the brain cells that make dopamine slowly die. Without dopamine, the cells that control movement can't send proper messages to the muscles, making it difficult to control the muscles. (Medline Plus, Medical Encyclopedia)

Micrographia: Small handwriting.

Neurotransmitter: A chemical signal that allows the billions of neurons in the nervous system to communicate with one another, making the nervous system the master communication system of the body. (Medline Plus, Medical Encyclopedia)

Parkinson's disease: A type of movement disorder that occurs when nerve cells in the brain don't produce enough of a brain chemical called dopamine. Sometimes it is genetic, but most cases do not seem to run in families. Exposure to chemicals in the environment might play a role. (NIH: National Institute of Neurological Disorders and Stroke)

Prodromal Symptom: A symptom indicating the early onset of a disease.

Let's Combat Micrographia[®] **Training Program and Instructor Training:**Visit www.letscombatmicrographia.com

DopaFit[®] **Parkinson's Movement Center and Program: For information on Parkinson's disease and exercise:** Visit www.dopafit.com

MedlinePlus: Trusted health information repository Visit https://medlineplus.gov

16
Let's Combat Micrographia® Workshop Graduate Testimonials

"After my handwriting became so cramped and small that I could no longer read it, I had no hope that I could ever recover it. After the first week of doing the Let's Combat Micrographia® exercises, I had to sign my name. The letters reminded me of a baby trying to walk for the first time. They were wobbly, but they were legible for the first time in years. This workshop has been an invaluable lifeline in my continued fight against my Parkinson's plus disease."—**Maryellen C.**

"When I took the class and did the assignments required, I was just flabbergasted with the results and that I was getting my groove back in my writing, and my self-esteem, along with my self-confidence, was at an all-time high that my fancy handwriting was coming back! Saba is truly a wonderful professor of Let's Combat Micrographia®! You can't go wrong—you can only go write!" —**Tim M.**

"I had always been proud of and complimented on my handwriting, but Parkinson's had turned it into something I didn't quite recognize as mine. After completing the micrographia workshop and utilizing the suggestions in the workbook, my handwriting looks like mine again. The practice sessions were 'key' in retraining the movement between brain and hand. I highly recommend the methods used to combat micrographia." —**Nancy M.**

"I took the micrographia workshop in conjunction with the DopaFit exercise class. The results were awesome! My son was so impressed with the results that he said, "I can actually read your writing." I keep my micrographia book with me at all times. When I feel I have been very busy and neglecting myself, my handwriting suffers and that is when I pull out the book and practice my writing. I am so ecstatic to have this at my fingertips. I know my handwriting has gone south, but I also know that with practice, it does get better."—**Gail N.**

17
About the Author

Saba M. Shahid is the CSO, or chief smiling officer, and president of The Art Cart. Saba was recently awarded the prestigious 40 Under 40 Award for her work with The Art Cart and lasting impact on the Parkinson's community. Saba has a master's degree in biomedical science from Quinnipiac University. While waiting for medical school admission, she combined her passion for medicine and art to establish The Art Cart's Smile Through Art® workshop curriculum with the goal of spreading smiles and healing through creativity and movement to every patient she has the privilege of interacting with. Soon after, Saba saw the need for introducing a curriculum to help people with Parkinson's disease improve their handwriting. Since 2014, Saba and her team have worked internationally to help thousands of people living with Parkinson's disease regain confidence in their abilities and find hope through both the Smile Through Art® curriculum and the Let's Combat Micrographia® curriculum.

Saba's husband, Chad Moir, is the CEO of DopaFit®, a Parkinson's-specific movement center that provides several different types of exercise therapies specifically developed for people living with Parkinson's disease. For more information on DopaFit®, please visit www.dopafit.com. For more information on The Art Cart, please visit www.smilethroughart.com.

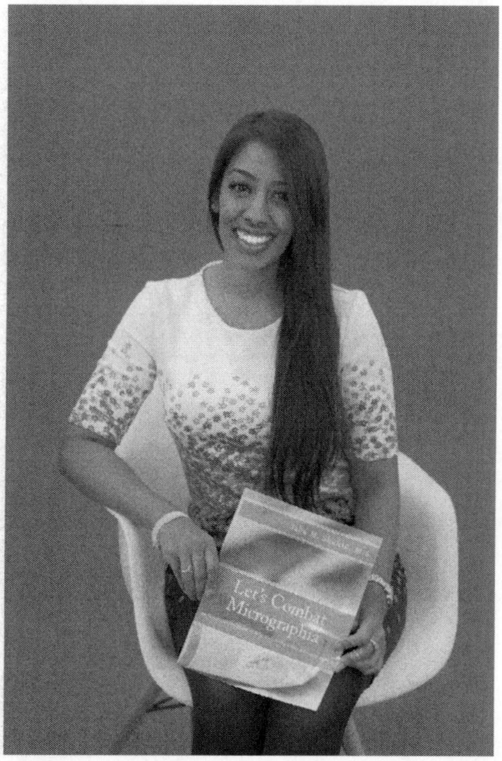
Let's Combat
Micrographia

Pictured above: Saba with the first edition of the

Let's Combat Micrographia® Workbook

Pictured below: Saba and her husband Chad

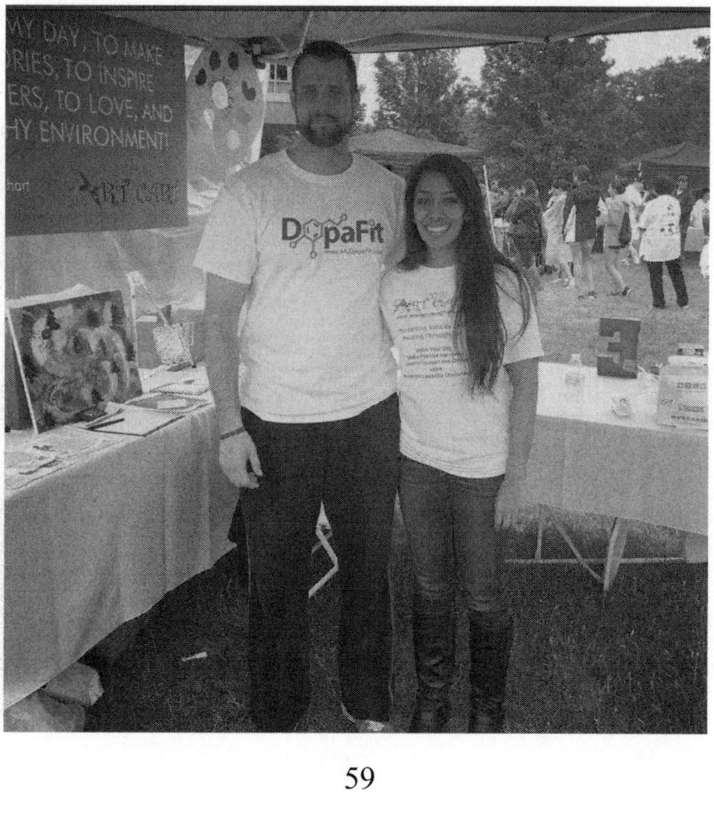
MY DAY, TO MAKE
RIES, TO INSPIRE
ERS, TO LOVE, AND
HY ENVIRONMENT!
DopaFit

SABA M. SHAHID, M.S.

Printed in Great Britain
by Amazon